BOOK ANALYSIS

By Cassandra Gibbons

The Underground Railroad

BY COLSON WHITEHEAD

BrightSummaries.com

COLSON WHITEHEAD

AMERICAN NOVELIST

- **Born in New York City in 1969.**
- **Notable works:**
    - *John Henry Days* (2001), novel
    - *The Colossus of New York* (2003), historical non-fiction
    - *Zone One* (2011), zombie novel

Colson Whitehead is an American novelist from New York. He grew up with three siblings in a very privileged household and studied at Harvard. Whilst there he took classes in theatre studies and African American studies because he found the English department to be too conservative, with a heavy focus on pre-20th century literature. After university, he decided to become a journalist and wrote for *The Village Voice* while writing what would become his first novel, *The Intuitionist*.

Whitehead was catapulted to fame with the 2016 publication of his sixth novel *The Underground*

Railroad. As a result, Whitehead was included in *Time* magazine's 2017 list of the 100 most influential people in the world. His article in *Time* was written by Oprah Winfrey, who had included *The Underground Railroad* in her influential book club. In between writing novels, Whitehead has taught creative writing at numerous institutions, including Princeton and NYU. His next novel, *The Nickel Boys*, is set in Jim Crow-era Florida and is due for publication in the summer of 2019. Whitehead has two children.

THE UNDERGROUND RAILROAD

A HISTORICAL NOVEL

- **Genre:** historical fiction
- **Reference edition:** Whitehead, C. (2016) *The Underground Railroad*. London: Little, Brown.
- **1st edition:** 2016
- **Themes:** slavery, African American history, violence, race, community

The Underground Railroad tells the story of Cora, a teenage girl and runaway slave, as she escapes her cotton plantation and makes her way north. The novel is divided into 12 chapters that are named after either characters or geographical locations (mostly states). The chapters named after states (and in one case, the North) detail Cora's time in each location, while the shorter chapters named after characters tell the backstory and fate (sometimes both) of said characters.

The novel is an example of the alternate history genre due to its literalisation of the Underground Railroad. This is a term used to describe the secret network that established routes and safe houses for escaped slaves in 19th-century America. In the novel, however, Whitehead depicts this network as being inclusive of a literal subterranean railway system, complete with trains. The novel became a number-one bestseller upon publication and won several literary awards, including the 2017 Pulitzer Prize for Fiction. It is set to be adapted into a television series.

SUMMARY

GEORGIA AND SOUTH CAROLINA

The novel begins with Caesar asking his fellow slave Cora to escape with him to the North. She initially says no, which is what her grandmother, Ajarry, would have done. Ajarry was taken from her native Africa to work on a cotton plantation, where she gave birth to five children. Only one, Mabel, survived into adulthood. Ajarry taught her children to be obedient in the hope that this would aid their survival. Mabel was not receptive to this message, and seemingly influenced her daughter in the same way. Cora says yes when Caesar asks her to run away with him the second time, and it is as if her mother, Mabel, is talking through her.

When Mabel escaped, Cora became an outcast, and was relegated to sleeping quarters with other outcasts called 'the Hob'. She has to fight to retain ownership of a small vegetable patch, which was passed down to her from her grandmother Ajarry via Mabel. Cora is gang raped in retribution. Despite being treated badly by her contemporaries, Cora contributes to the community and even defends Chester, a young boy who accidentally knocks into Terrance Randall, one of the owners of the plantation. Both Cora and Chester are badly beaten. Terrance becomes the sole owner of the plantation when his kinder brother James dies, and asserts his power by killing a runaway slave, Big Anthony, in a grotesque fashion – by maiming him and then roasting him alive.

The increase in violence convinces Cora to escape with Caesar. They are followed by Cora's friend Lovey, but are then ambushed by four white men. Lovey is detained by them and taken back to the plantation, but Cora and Caesar manage to fight off their attackers. Cora's attacker sustains serious head injuries and later dies. Cora and Caesar manage to get to a safe house, from which they are taken to the Underground Railroad by Mr Fletcher, a white ally. They take the train and emerge in South Carolina. Meanwhile, a slave catcher called Ridgeway has been hired by Terrance Randall to track Cora down.

Cora and Caesar settle comfortably in South Carolina under new identities and decide to stay, eschewing trains going further north. All is not as it seems, however, and Cora soon learns that the apparent benevolence of the South Carolinians is masking a sinister programme to sterilise African Americans. She is offered sterilisation and told, truthfully, that it is her choice, but it is clear that other women are not given the choice. She goes from a happy job working as a nanny to a living model in the African section of a museum. Cora finally goes back to the Underground Railroad station when she realises that Ridgeway has caught up with her, but Caesar is not warned in time, and is recaptured. The station agent Sam's house, which is above the rail station, is burnt down.

NORTH CAROLINA AND TENNESSEE

Cora manages to stop a train and get on, but is told by the driver that the Georgia station has closed down and that he was not expecting a passenger. He drops her in North Carolina and can take her no further. When Cora is collected by the station agent, Martin, she is horrified to discover that North Carolina is in the process of killing its black population, hoping to replaced black slaves with Irish and German immigrants.

She sees the victims of this genocide swinging from the trees on her way to Martin's house, where she is stowed in a nook of the attic. From a small hole in the wall she can see the weekly spectacles in the park, which consist of blackface sketches for entertainment, followed by the public lynching of a black person.

Cora stays in the attic for several months. She continues with her education (she was given rudimentary reading lessons in South Carolina) by reading Martin's almanacs and the Bible. Martin's wife Ethel disapproves of Cora, fearing repercussions should she be found, but nurses the girl back to health when Cora falls ill. Martin and Ethel's Irish maid, Fiona, tells the authorities that she suspects they are harbouring a runaway, and is paid for her information. Cora is dragged out of the house and Martin and Ethel are tied to the tree that is normally used to hang black people. The townspeople begin to throw rocks at them. Cora is spared immediate death only by the reappearance of Ridgeway, who takes her away with the intention of returning her to Randall's plantation and claiming his reward.

Ridgeway takes Cora on the beginnings of the journey back to Georgia. In tow are Jasper, another escaped slave, Boseman, an associate of Ridgeway, and Ridgeway's young black assistant, Homer. Ridgeway bought Homer's freedom but Homer does not know how to live as a free man, and so continues working for Ridgeway, even putting chains on when he sleeps at night. Ridgeway is irritated by Jasper's constant singing, and shoots him, deciding that the reward does not justify the hassle of keeping him alive. Ridgeway tells a horrified Cora about Lovey's slow death back at the plantation.

Their journey takes them through Tennessee, where they come across fields that have been razed to the ground and communities that have been struck with yellow fever. Ridgeway takes Cora to an inn to eat and tells her about Caesar's death. Cora is better prepared than she was when he told her about Lovey as she had already told herself that Caesar must have died, and processed the information. She manages to remain impassive. Later that night, the group are stopped by three free men, who kill Boseman, chain Ridgeway up and free Cora.

INDIANA AND THE NORTH

Cora is taken to John Valentine's Farm in Indiana, where she finds peace. She resumes her education, has comfortable lodgings that she shares with two other women and begins to develop a relationship with Royal, one of the free men who rescued her. He brings her almanacs to help her learn how to read and Cora opens up to him about her life on the plantation. The three dominating figures on the farm are John Valentine himself, who purchased his wife Gloria's freedom; Elijah Lander, a light-skinned biracial speechmaker; and Mingo, a black resident of the farm who favours driving out runaways like Cora.

Cora makes the decision to stay on in Indiana, but worries that she may regret it, like she did in South Carolina. She is comforted by a visit from Sam, who tells her that Terrance Randall has died and there is nothing to suggest that the new owner of the plantation will pursue Cora. Nevertheless, Cora is unable to fully relax. She has a conversation in the library with John Valentine, who shares her concerns. The white population of Indiana is, he thinks, bound to be uncomfortable with such a large, educated black community. He fears that this former-slaver state will try to subdue the farm in order to eliminate the possibility of a black rebellion.

Shortly after this conversation, the community gathers to hear Mingo and Lander speak. Mingo argues that the community should expel runaways, particularly those accused of crimes (he looks pointedly at Cora when he says this), and that all links with the Underground Railroad should be severed in order to preserve the farm. Lander disagrees, and argues that they should help as many people as they can. At this point the gathering is interrupted by a baying mob who shoot and kill Lander, and also Royal. It is strongly suspected that Mingo arranged the attack. In the chaos, Cora is once again captured by Ridgeway, who orders her to show him the Underground Railroad.

Cora regrets never telling Royal that she loved him, and hopes that he knew. She leads Ridgeway and Homer to the Underground Railroad after being threatened with a pistol and opens the hatch to the station platform. She grabs onto Ridgeway's body and the two of them tumble down the stairs. Ridgeway bears the brunt of the fall, breaking his leg badly and sustaining serious head injuries. While Homer attends to him, Cora makes her escape into the tunnel on a handcar, which she eventually abandons in favour of walking. She emerges into the light and is picked up by a free man driving a cart. He gives her some food and tells her he is heading west to California. She wonders how far he has come, and what he has escaped from.

CHARACTER STUDY

CORA

Cora is a teenage girl who was born into slavery on a cotton plantation in Georgia. When she is ten or eleven (she does not know her exact age), her mother, Mabel, escapes the plantation without her. Cora's feelings towards her mother are a mixture of disgust and admiration. She is furious that her mother would abandon her to her fate but also inspired by the fact that she managed to do it. Her mother's apparent success in escaping spurs Cora on to achieve the same ambition. Wherever Cora goes after her escape, she asks people if they know of a Mabel from Georgia. She fantasises about her mother living in abject poverty, but never fantasises about her having died, the more probable and indeed true outcome, suggesting that she still, on some level, cares for her mother.

Cora is characterised by a worrisome distrust of everyone she meets. She is so surprised to be treated with respect in South Carolina and

Indiana that she suspects it is too good to be true, and in both cases it is. Cruelly, her life in both places is upended just when she has begun to relax a little and enjoy her freedom. Her relationships with men are impaired by her violent sexual assault a few years earlier. She rebuffs Caesar's advances, although she thinks that she might have returned his feelings after a little time had passed. She begins to trust men again enough to kiss Royal, but is unable to tell him that she loves him or consummate the relationship before his untimely death. When she finally reaches the North, she ignores white passersby, even one who offers to help her, and accepts food only from a black passerby.

Cora's will to survive and, in some parts, sheer luck drives the plot forward. Her interactions with secondary characters allow Whitehead to tell not only her story, but also this multitude of peripheral stories at the same time. The novel's depiction of multiple characters allows it to paint an accurate picture of life in the antebellum South. While Cora's relationship with her mother is a significant part of the novel, her cat and mouse interaction with Ridgeway is also integral to the plot. Cora's confidence grows with each escape, and when she is captured by Ridgeway for a second time, she learns how to deal with him and finally finds the strength to overpower him and cause his literal downfall.

MABEL

Mabel is Cora's mother, and like her daughter was born into slavery on the Randall cotton plantation in Georgia. She was taught by her mother to be obedient and keep her head down in order to survive. When Cora is ten or eleven, Mabel disappears, and it is assumed that she has successfully escaped. For much of the novel the reader is led to believe that Mabel selfishly left her daughter behind. It is only in the penultimate chapter that the reader learns the truth, although Cora never does. Mabel did consider escaping, but stopped a few miles away from the plantation and headed back in order to be with her daughter. On her return, however, she was fatally bitten by a snake and her body was engulfed by the swamp.

Mabel acts as a shining example in the novel, before her true fate is revealed, of a successful escape, but she is also castigated for leaving her daughter behind. She clearly inspires her daughter, while simultaneously inspiring hatred. She also makes Ridgeway more vigorous in his pursuit of Cora: he is determined that she will not outwit him as Mabel did. Whitehead's decision to reveal Mabel's fate in the penultimate chapter completely changes the reader's perception of her, and also contextualises her behaviour. She did seriously consider leaving, but was driven to do so by the repeated rapes that she submitted to because her attacker, Moses, threatened to rape Cora if Mabel resisted. Mabel was, ultimately, driven by her love for her daughter.

RIDGEWAY

Ridgeway is the slave catcher hired by Terrance Randall to track Cora down. Having been unsuccessful in his previous attempt to track Mabel down, Ridgeway is determined to find Cora and maintain his reputation as a top slave catcher. He is unapologetically racist, and often refers to black people as 'it', to emphasise his opinion that black people are not people at all:

> "Ridgeway slurped. 'We caught up with it [Caesar] at the factory at the end of its shift... They broke into the jail and ripped its body to pieces.'" (p. 219)

Ridgeway plays the role of the antagonist. He continues to pursue Cora even after Terrance Randall dies, which means that if he returns Cora to the plantation he might not be paid; he wants to catch Cora out of spite and pride. His reputation as a slave catcher is in tatters when Cora escapes his clutches. He has a high sense of self-importance, as evidenced by his insistence that his assistant, Homer, write down his final thoughts before he dies.

CAESAR

Caesar is, like Cora, a slave, but he has benefitted from a relatively kind mistress who taught him how to read and promised him and his family freedom upon her death. She did not leave a will expressing this wish, however, and so Caesar was sold when she died and ended up on the Randall plantation. He tells Cora that he asked her to escape with him because her mother managed to flee successfully. In a later chapter titled 'Caesar', the reader learns that he actually wanted to escape with her after seeing her defend Chester. He plays an important part in driving the plot forward because he successfully convinces Cora to leave with him. He is characterised by his resilience, intelligence and caring nature.

ANALYSIS

HISTORICAL FICTION AND THE 'ALTERNATE HISTORY' GENRE

The Underground Railroad conforms to the historical fiction genre in its accurate representation of the antebellum South. This is evident not only in its setting but in the attention to detail regarding objects and vehicles and authentic dialogue. Cora's language reflects her lack of education, whereas Caesar, who has a benevolent mistress who allowed him to be educated, makes fewer grammatical errors. Whitehead does not shy away from the liberal use of terms like 'pickaninny', the usage of which is historically justified despite the offensiveness of the word in a modern context. The future status of the term as offensive is foreshadowed when Cora is told by her teacher in Indiana not to use it.

While the novel is broadly historically accurate, the eponymous Underground Railroad is literalised and given a new, historically false, presence. While the term historically referred to the network of safe houses and routes used to smuggle slaves from the South into the free states of the North, in the novel Whitehead turns it into a literal subterranean railway network. It is the literalising of this metaphor that makes the alternate history genre applicable to this novel. The alternate history genre normally poses 'what if...?' questions designed to speculate about an alternative history in which an event happened differently to how it happened in real life.

In *The Underground Railroad*, this 'what if...?' question does not particularly lead to a huge change in circumstance. The novel poses the following question: what if the Underground Railroad literally referred to a subterranean railway, even though such a thing did not exist in the early stages of the 19th century in which the novel is set? The answer that Whitehead suggests is that things would not have been so different. The network would still have been difficult to operate, given the immense security and secrecy needed to maintain such an operation, and so the railroad would not necessarily have rescued slaves in greater numbers had it consisted of actual trains. The lack of difference between the novel and historical reality is the reason why the novel does not fall under the speculative genre (a genre closely tied with alternate history).

The Underground Railroad of the novel still conforms historically to the actual Underground Railroad in many ways. The station agents and train drivers are a mixture of abolitionist allies and free former slaves, for example. Network operators are given the minimum amount of information to work their section of the railroad. Royal, for example, cannot tell Cora who built the railroad, nor where exactly it leads. The train driver who takes Cora to North Carolina tells her that he was not expecting any passengers and that he thinks the Georgia station has been closed down. But he cannot know for sure because extreme levels of secrecy were maintained (both in the novel and in real life) in order to prevent widespread damage should the network be infiltrated.

CHAPTER STRUCTURE

The novel consists of 12 chapters, six of which are named after characters, six of which are named after states. The novel is structured to alternate between the character chapters and the state chapters. The chapters named after states are longer, and most of them are divided into sub-chapters. They follow Cora as she experiences the different ways in which each state treats black people, varying from the barbarism of Georgia and North Carolina to the tentative, if short-lived, sympathy of South Carolina and Indiana. The chapters named after characters, on the other hand, are much shorter and focus on the backstory, motivations, and sometimes fate of the eponymous character.

In some cases, the character chapter follows the state chapter in which said character featured prominently. This is the case particularly with Ethel and Stevens. The latter is a doctor who offers Cora sterilisation. The short chapter detailing how he uses black bodies to practice on over white bodies highlights his dehumanisation of black people. This characteristic, which is touched upon in the South Carolina chapter, is emphasised in his character chapter. Ethel, on the other hand, is largely presented as cold and mean-spirited in the state chapter in which she features prominently, North Carolina. But her character chapter shows her to have had a black friend when growing up, whom her family dissuaded her from spending time with. Her ultimately sympathetic but warped experiences of having relationships with black people are the reason for her odd treatment of Cora. Her character chapter is intended to shed light on the inner workings of her mind.

Caesar's chapter, on the other hand, appears long after his character has died in South Carolina. His chapter comes after Tennessee, in which Cora is told by Ridgeway that Caesar has died. Cora has already accepted that Caesar cannot have made it out alive, but the finality of his death triggers a chapter to examine his character a little more. In this way, both Cora and the reader have some sort of closure over Caesar's death. It is revealed that Caesar went to the schoolhouse back on Randall's plantation not to have sex with women, but to illicitly study his books. A quirk of his character that had earlier made Cora distrust him (she took him to be a womaniser) is explained and it alters the reader's perception of Caesar.

Finally, the last character chapter focuses on Mabel's story, and informs the reader of her true fate, which Cora will tragically never find out. This chapter is strategically placed at the end to allow the reader to build up a negative perception of Mabel, whom Cora criticises throughout the novel, which is then completely overturned when the reader learns that Mabel ultimately decided not to escape without her daughter. She was unable to get back to her due to a fatal snakebite, and her body was engulfed by the swamp. Given that Mabel is such an important driver of plot in the novel, motivating Cora to escape and Ridgeway to catch mother and daughter, this clarifying of events changes the reader's perception of the events of the entire novel.

SLAVERY

The central theme of *The Underground Railroad* is slavery, and Whitehead uses brutal imagery to depict the violence and horror faced by slaves in the South in the antebellum era. Aside from beatings, floggings and brandings, the deaths of attempted runaways are depicted in gruesome detail. Not only are the deaths depicted, they are also portrayed as entertainment for white people, as in the case of Big Anthony's death, which is preceded by days of torture. The image is haunting not only for its vivid depiction of violence, but also because it is the fate that awaits Cora should she be caught and returned to Randall's plantation:

> "Randall's visitors sipped spiced rum as Big Anthony was doused with oil and roasted. The witnesses were spared his screams, as his manhood had been cut off on the first day, stuffed in his mouth, and sewn in." (p. 47)

Beyond the violence, the injustices of slavery are frequently represented. Caesar is verbally promised his freedom by his relatively kind mistress but is sold by her relatives when her benevolent promise is not backed up by any will. When he is sold, he is split up from his family and given only moments to say goodbye to them. Cora does not know her exact age because her birth was not considered important enough to mark by noting down the date. When Terrance takes over his brother James' half of the plantation, he imposes arbitrary rules such as the ending of Christmas celebrations. He also inspects the teeth of a young boy, "wrenching the boy's jaw to get a good look" (*ibid.*) as if the boy is not a human at all, but rather an animal owned by Terrance. This is an example of the constant dehumanisation faced by the slaves throughout the novel. They are often referred to as 'property' in a similar fashion.

The novel does not, however, shy away from depicting violence and hatred within the slave community. Cora is gang raped by slaves after defending her plot of land, and is shunned by the community as an outsider on the say so of another slave, Ava. The novel often presents a distinct lack of solidarity in the community, which is intentional on the part of Whitehead. He has stated in an interview that he believes people who were tortured, raped and dehumanised would most likely lash out at those around them (Brockes, 2017). Depictions of camaraderie in historical fiction depicting slaves are too idealistic and sugar-coated, in his opinion. In presenting enmity between the slaves, Whitehead honestly depicts the reality of living in such a toxic environment, and the inevitable effects such living would have on the concept of community.

FURTHER REFLECTION

SOME QUESTIONS TO THINK ABOUT...

- Discuss the growth of Cora's character as the novel progresses.
- Discuss the characters of Miss Lucy and Dr Stevens. Are their attitudes ultimately favourable towards black people? Explain your answer.
- Discuss how Mabel's actions both help and hinder her daughter.
- Do the chapters focusing on minor characters interrupt the flow of the plot or aid the telling of the story?
- "There was only darkness outside the windows on her journeys, and only ever would be darkness." (p. 263) Is this an accurate description of Cora's life?
- Compare *The Underground Railroad* to another novel you have read, or a film you have watched, that deals with slavery.
- In your opinion, is the character Ridgeway beyond redemption? Explain your answer.
- How might the novel have been different if Cora had been a man?

We want to hear from you!
Leave a comment on your online library
and share your favourite books on social media!

FURTHER READING

REFERENCE EDITION

- Whitehead, C. (2016) *The Underground Railroad*. London: Little, Brown.

REFERENCE STUDIES

- Brockes, E. (2017) Interview: Colson Whitehead. *The Guardian*. [Online]. [Accessed 17 February 2019]. Available from: <https://www.theguardian.com/books/2017/jul/07/colson-whitehead-underground-railroad>

www.brightsummaries.com

Ebook EAN: 9782808018593

Paperback EAN: 9782808018609

Legal Deposit: D/2019/12603/96

Cover: © Primento

Digital conception by Primento, the digital partner of publishers.

Printed in Great Britain
by Amazon

61519750R00031